The Aboriginal Population Of Alameda And Contra Costa Counties, California

by

S. F. Cook

The Aboriginal Population Of Alameda And Contra Costa Counties, California
by S. F. Cook

ISBN: 978-93-59957-56-2

Published by

DOUBLE 9 BOOKS

2/13-B, Ansari Road
Daryaganj, New Delhi – 110002
info@double9books.com
www.double9books.com
Tel. 011-40042856

ABOUT THE AUTHOR

S. F. Cook, the accomplished creator of "The Aboriginal Population of Alameda and Contra Costa Counties, California," stands as a high-quality determine inside the realm of historical and demographic literature. This work is frequently appeared as considered one of his masterpieces, reflecting his determination to bridging the nation-states of history and demography. With a notable pen and a profound expertise of his subjects, Cook excels in elucidating the complex historical and demographic elements of the indigenous populations in Alameda and Contra Costa Counties. His writings transcend mere data and information, facilitating a deeper connection amongst readers and fostering a superior understanding of both the past and the folks who inhabit those areas. Cook's literary prowess is a testomony to his creativity and ardour. He invitations readers on a fascinating journey thru numerous landscapes and emotions, painting vibrant pix together with his phrases. His writing style is a brilliant fusion of beauty and accessibility, making his extraordinary tales a satisfaction for readers of all backgrounds and interests. S. F. Cook's contributions to the literary global expand beyond his understanding in historical and demographic studies; his capacity to train, inspire, and connect people via the pages of his books ensures that his legacy endures as an enriching and enlightening pressure within the world of literature.

CONTENTS

INTRODUCTION

The following pages have a twofold purpose. First, there is extended to new territory an analysis of aboriginal population and ecology in California which has already encompassed the San Joaquin Valley (Cook, 1955) and the north coast (Cook, 1956). The area treated here is a portion of that occupied by the Costanoan linguistic division, which extended from San Francisco Bay throughout the interior ranges and along the coast as far south as the latitude of Salinas and Monterey. However, in view of the many accounts which have been written concerning the settlement of coastal California and the establishment of the missions, it seems preferable to devote attention almost exclusively to one restricted region and to deal with this as exhaustively as possible. The area selected embraces the east shore of San Francisco Bay and its hinterland, including what is now Alameda and Contra Costa counties. It is quite true that some of the tribal groups inhabiting this territory may not have been members of the Costanoan stock. On the other hand, in their relation both to the native environment and to the invading white man their activity conformed in all important ways to that of their bona fide Costanoan neighbors. Hence it is proper to treat all the aborigines in the area on a common basis.

Second, emphasis has been placed upon setting forth in detail sources of knowledge. There are a number of documents describing conditions in the East Bay from 1770 to 1820. Certain of these, such as the Crespi-Fages and the Font-Anza diaries, have been made available in excellent translations, particularly by Herbert E. Bolton, and although they must be examined and analyzed with care, only a few passages need to be reproduced verbatim. Other documents, some of them of considerable general interest, are almost unknown, not only to students of ethnography, but also to many others concerned with preconquest and early colonial California. Among these may be mentioned the Cañizares exploration of San Francisco Bay, and the diaries of Father Danti and Sergeant Amador. Therefore, although a good deal of the material contained in these documents does not bear directly upon either population or ecology, it seems to me worth while to translate and reproduce them in full. Their intrinsic interest is adequate compensation for the moderate amount of extra space consumed.

THE FAGES-CRESPI EXPEDITION

The earliest land explorations to Alameda and Contra Costa counties were those of Fages in 1772 and of Anza in 1776. Journals were kept of both these trips; for the first by Crespi, for the second, by Anza himself and also by Font. All are well known and are easily available in the excellent translations by Herbert E. Bolton (1927; 1930). Therefore only the significant points are abstracted and referred to here.

Coming up from Monterey, the Fages-Crespi expedition camped (Bolton, 1927, p. 284) on March 24, 1772, near Milpitas. On March 25 the party moved north along the plain, which is described as being well-covered with grass but treeless, as far as San Lorenzo Creek. Five villages of natives were seen, situated on as many creeks, all concentrated within three leagues.

On March 26 the region of Fruitvale was reached (Bolton [1927, p. 287] says Mills College). Many deer were seen and also the tracks of elk. In the four leagues traversed, five streams of running water were found, and the vicinity of the Oakland-Alameda Estuary is noted as being covered with oaks. No Indians were seen. On the 27th, after crossing a grassy plain, the party reached Strawberry Creek. Seven arroyos were crossed, but again no Indians were seen. On the 28th the party reached Pinole. Six arroyos were crossed. At two leagues they reached Wildcat Creek where "... we found a good village of heathen, very fair and bearded ... they gave us many cacomites, amoles and two dead geese, dried and stuffed with grass to use as decoys in hunting others, large numbers being attracted in this way" (Bolton, 1927, p. 291).

On March 29, Crespi and Fages continued along the shore, reaching the western end of Carquinez Strait, "traveling by treeless, grass-covered hills." They continued along the steep bluffs on the south side, probably nearly to Martinez. "In the whole distance we traveled on these hills there was not a single tree. The bed of the estuary is very deep and its shores precipitous; on its banks we did not see so much as a bush ..." The last statement is interesting in view of the evidence contained in the accounts of Font and Anza .

Several native villages were seen. "On the banks of the other side we made out many villages, whose Indians called to us ... and many of them, seeing that we were going away, came to this side, crossing over on rafts, and gave us some of their wild food." On the south side: "In this part of our day's march we came to five large villages of very wild heathen ..." It is probable that the expression "this part of the day's march" refers to the first portion, i.e., from Pinole through Rodeo and Crockett. There the natives had "... pleasant faces, and were of a fair complexion, bearded and white, all with long hair which they tied with twine."

On March 30 the expedition set out and in two leagues crossed Pacheco Creek (see Bolton, 1927, p. 295n), which was a "deep arroyo with much running water" and bordered with trees. This reference to "running water" raises the question of local water supply, a matter that will be discussed more fully in connection with the Font-Anza descriptions. The plain between Walnut Creek and Concord is described as being well covered with grass and grown with oak trees. In this valley two Indian villages were encountered. After crossing the low hills northwest of Concord, Crespi and Fages entered the delta region of the Central Valley and camped somewhere near Pittsburg or Antioch.

The next day, March 31, it was decided to return. Accordingly, the steps of the preceding day were retraced as far as the area of Walnut Creek, whence they turned south to the night's camp near Danville. (This itinerary has been worked out by Bolton and is no doubt substantially correct.) On April 1 the party reached Pleasanton via San Ramon and Dublin, and on April 2 arrived near Milpitas.

The valley at and south of Walnut Creek is described as being covered with grass with the stream beds overgrown with alders, cottonwood, laurels, roses, and other shrubs. The same type of land, "covered with grass and trees," continued as far as Pleasanton. Then: "It is evident that the land is not so good now, but it all continues full of oaks and live oaks...." Crossing the hills to the shore of the Bay the same rough, wooded country persisted — essentially as it is today.

During the three days many signs of natives were encountered. Near Walnut Creek "we came to three villages with some little grass houses...." Between Danville and Pleasanton there were "numerous villages of very gentle and peaceful heathen, many of them of fair complexion." From Pleasanton to the Bay no new villages or Indians are mentioned.

From Milpitas north, Crespi saw five villages, as far as San Lorenzo. In Oakland and Berkeley he saw none. There was one "good village" on Wildcat Creek and from Pinole to Crockett there were five "large villages." In lower Walnut Creek Valley there were two more. The total is thirteen, and it is surprising that no more were encountered. Possibly the party kept too far inland to see the shell midden sites along the Bay shore.

With reference to numbers of natives it should be remembered that Crespi had seen Indian rancherias ranging in size from insignificant to the semi-cities of the Santa Barbara Channel. Hence a "large village" to him must have meant a really sizable place. If we ascribe 100 inhabitants to an ordinary village and 200 to a "large" or "good" village, we get a total of 1,900 persons.

On the return trip through the interior hills Crespi notes three villages near Walnut Creek and numerous villages in the vicinity of Livermore Valley. If we allow "numerous" to be half a dozen, there is a total of nine villages. The size was likely to be smaller than on the Bay shore, say 50 persons. Then the total population represented would be 400-500. For those portions of Alameda and Contra Costa counties visited a population of at least 2,400 is therefore indicated. Since Crespi probably did not see all the villages, the actual value was no doubt considerably greater.

THE ANZA-FONT EXPEDITION

Attention should be directed now to the Anza expedition, which reached the East Bay in late March, 1776. The three accounts will be considered collectively for present purposes and will be designated A (Anza's Diary), F1 (Font's Short Diary), and F2 (Font's Complete Diary). Since this expedition was—with all deference to the efforts of Fray Crespi—much more carefully and exhaustively recorded than the Fages trip of 1772, it merits extended citation and analysis.

If Bolton's reconstruction is correct (1930, III: 133, 263; IV: 352), the Anza expedition, having come down the peninsula from San Francisco, halted for the evening March 30, 1776, near Agnew, between Alviso and Santa Clara. The following day, March 31, they crossed the Coyote River about two miles south of Warm Springs and moved north and northwest as far as San Lorenzo Creek.

They remained close to the hills, apparently, for Anza (A) says, "The road runs close to a small range completely bare of trees, for none are seen except some which grow in the canyons." After leaving Coyote Creek, Anza (A) encountered an arroyo, "which has plenty of trees and has water in abundance ... ," probably Mission Creek or Alameda Creek. Thereafter they crossed four arroyos "with little water," the last one of which was San Lorenzo Creek. Font (F2) states that after having passed a "salty lagoon" (north of Irvington) they crossed five arroyos.

During the day the party saw six villages, says Anza (A), most of whose habitants had fled. On the other hand, about 40 "heathen" were met along the road. Font (F2) is much more informative than Anza. All along the plain they saw "occasional Indians." Those whom they met before reaching the "first arroyo" (probably Alameda Creek near Niles)

> ... appear to be very poor and miserable, for they have not even firewood by which to keep warm, and they go about naked ... and eat grass and herbs and some roots like medium-sized onions, which they call amole, and in which those plains greatly abound. One Indian who carried his provisions on the end of a pole invited us to eat some of them.

On or near Alameda Creek they met "about thirty Indians" (Anza says 40), who greeted them peaceably. Font here notes that "their language is distinct from all those we had formerly heard and is very ugly; and with the gobbling which they made, all speaking together, it was very disagreeable to the ears." Font also comments in another place on the language: "The Indians whom we saw along here are totally distinct in language from the previous ones." Since the Spaniards had been in Costanoan territory for many days, they must have encountered a sharp dialectic boundary at the southeastern corner of San Francisco Bay. Both Anza and Font (F2) describe the incidents of this encounter in graphic terms.

Two leagues beyond the creek (somewhere near Alvarado) a village without people was seen. Then:

> We traveled a league more and crossed another arroyo, where we saw an abandoned village, and in a hut many birds stuffed with grass, which some Indians had to hunt with. Here the soldiers got some wild tobacco of which there was a considerable amount.

Although Font does not mention the exact number of villages seen, his account in other respects closely parallels that of Anza and does nothing to refute the statement that there were six villages between Irvington and San Lorenzo.

On the appearance of these Indians Font and Anza are very positive. Crespi had said the natives were light-colored. Font says (F2, p. 356), "They are somewhat bearded, gentle, and very poor, but in color they are the same as all the rest." Elsewhere he reiterates his opinion that Crespi was mistaken. Anza adds, regarding appearance (A, p. 136):

> The Indians who have been seen from the first arroyo forward are not short haired like those from the Mission of San Antonio to the port of San Francisco. These of which we are now speaking wear their hair tied upon the very top of their heads where only a piece of thread is to be seen.

The journey on April 1 brought Anza's party to camp on Rodeo Creek (Bolton, 1930, II: 138n). It is noteworthy that these explorers saw much more timber than had Crespi, or perhaps they were merely more circumstantial in their account. Font (F2) says:

> The road followed the foot hills of the range which I mentioned on the 8th of March. In all its exterior this range

has very few trees, except a grove of redwoods in front of
the mouth of the port, although in its interior it has thickly
grown groves and is quite broken ...

Anza notes also "a large grove of pines of redwoods." Alameda Island is described as having "a very thick grove of oaks and live oaks on the banks of the estuary." The same grove is shown on Font's sketch of the area (Bolton, 1930, IV: 362) with the legend: "Bosque que esta al estsudeste de la Boca del Puerto."

On some of the streams there is said to be a prolific growth of trees, on others very little. Thus Font (F2) says that San Leandro Creek (Bolton's identification) had "a very deep bed grown with cottonwoods, live oaks, laurels and other trees." The creek near Mills College was "almost without trees." Somewhere in Oakland the party crossed two arroyos with "a heavy growth of trees." North of Oakland the vegetation apparently varied. The general impression one gets is that the larger streams were bordered by oak, willow, and cottonwood, whereas the smaller ones were essentially destitute of trees.

The Spaniards had considerable contact this day with the natives. Font in the Complete Diary makes it clear that Oakland and Berkeley were crossed and Wildcat Creek reached before the first Indians were seen. At that point, however, an abandoned village was found. On the banks of the next arroyo was an inhabited village containing 23 men and 7 women, others being away foraging. Anza says this was a village of about 100 persons. Font then says that on the next arroyo was a "fair-sized village." Although Anza does not specifically mention this village, both he and Font agree that at the camp (on Rodeo Creek) was another town, which Anza says "is larger than the two mentioned." Font concurs, in effect, with the statement that when the expedition halted, they were greeted by 38 Indians—presumably adult males.

Both authors comment on customs. Anza emphasizes the fact that these Indians are not white, in contradistinction to the reports brought back by Crespi. He also says the language is different "from that on the other side of the southern estuary." Font describes the people at the second inhabited village, who

> ... were very happy to see us and very obliging. They
> presented us with many cacomites, which is a little bulb or
> root almost round and rather flat, and the size and shape of
> a somewhat flattened ball, and likewise with a good string

of roasted amole, which is another root like a rather long onion, all well cooked and roasted ... The amole, which is their most usual food, tastes a little like mescal. It is the food which most abounds, and the fields along here are full of it.

Font (F2) adds the following description of the natives seen at the final halt on Rodeo Creek:

As soon as we halted thirty-eight Indians came to us unarmed, peaceful, and very happy to see us. At first they stopped and sat down on a small hill near the camp. Then one came, and behind him another, and so they came in single file like a flock of goats, leaping and talking, until all had arrived. They were very obliging, bringing us firewood, and very talkative, their language having much gobbling, nothing of which we understood. They go naked like all the rest, and they are by no means white, but are like all those whom we saw on the other side near the mouth of the port. After they had been a while with us they bade us goodby and we made signs to them that they should go and get us some fish with two hooks which I gave them. They apparently understood us clearly, but they brought us nothing and showed very little appreciation for the hooks, because their method of fishing is with nets.

On Tuesday, April 2, the Anza expedition continued along the southeast shore of San Pablo Bay, the south bank of Carquinez Strait, and halted on Walnut Creek, near Pacheco (the place called Santa Angela de Fulgino by Crespi). Water was scarce; no mention is made of crossing any creeks during the march until they arrived at Walnut Creek in the evening.

The descriptions of the vegetation along Carquinez Strait are somewhat ambiguous. It will be remembered that the impression given by Crespi for this stretch is one of total absence of trees. Anza says (A):

... for half a league up the river [by which he means Carquinez Strait] we kept very close to the Sierra which we have had on our right and which we skirted until yesterday. And we now again came to have it on the same side, so improved in abundance of firewood, and timber of oak and live oak that all its canyons are well provided with one and the other, the very opposite of what is seen on the other side of the river

[i.e., the north shore of the strait], where in four leagues we
have not seen a single tree.

In describing the strait Font (F2) says:

> In some places its banks are very precipitous, and in others it
> has a narrow beach on which, near its mouth [i.e. the western
> end], there are great piles of fresh-water mussels. The hills
> which form this channel are without trees, but those on this
> side have plentiful pasturage, while those on the other side
> appeared bald, with little grass, the earth being reddish in
> color.

During the afternoon the party traveled from the vicinity of Crockett "two leagues east along the top of the hills close to the water, and one east-southeast up the canyon which had some oaks and other trees, by which we again came out at the top of the hills near the water." According to Bolton (1930, IV: 375n), this point was on the bluffs just west of Martinez.

The implication of Anza's account and the rather specific statement by Font seem to support Crespi's description. There was little oak or other type of woody plant on the south shore west of what is now Port Costa. From there to Martinez the canyons held a fair growth of oak. In those areas not bearing oak, the primary plant cover was grass. Neither Crespi nor Anza nor Font gives any hint of the heavy infiltration of shrubby vegetation, such as *Baccharis*, poison oak, or other chapparal species, which now extend down the entire slope of the hills from Crockett to Martinez. The deduction is reasonable, although strict proof is lacking, that the modern vegetation has entered the region since 1775.

On this day Anza and Font made the acquaintance of two new species of fish, the sturgeon and the salmon, good descriptions of which are recorded by both explorers. Furthermore, the day was notable for encounters with the natives. Shortly after breaking camp the Spaniards were met by ten Indians who invited them to the nearby village (which Bolton says was at Tormey, about 2 miles west of Crockett). This village was large; Font estimated the population as 400 persons and Anza as 500. Font's account (F2) of his visit is long and circumstantial, but its value for ethnographic detail is such that it merits reproduction in full:

> Their method of welcoming us was like this: at sunrise the
> ten Indians came, one behind another, singing and dancing.
> One carried the air, making music with a little stick, rather
> long and split in the middle, which he struck against his

hand and which sounded something like a castanet. They reached the camp and continued their singing and dancing for a little while. Then they stopped dancing, all making a step in unison, shaking the body and saying dryly and in one voice, "Ha, ha, ha!" Next they sat down on the ground and signalled to us that we must sit down also. So we sat down in front of them, the commander, I, and the commissary. Now an Indian arose and presented the commander with a string of cacomites, and again sat down. Shortly afterward he rose again and made me a present of another string of cacomites, and again sat down. In this way they went making us their little presents, another Indian giving me a very large root of chuchupate which he began to eat, telling me by signs that it was good.

This compliment being over, they invited us to go to their village, indicating that it was nearby. The commander consented to give them this pleasure, and at once we began to travel. They followed after us with their singing and dancing.... After going a short distance we came to the village, which was in a little valley on the bank of a small arroyo, the Indians welcoming us with an indescribable hullabaloo. Three of them came to the edge of the village with some long poles with feathers on the end, and some long and narrow strips of skin with the hair on, which looked to me like rabbit skin, hanging like a pennant, this being their sign of peace. They led us to the middle of the village where there was a level spot like a plaza, and then began to dance with other Indians of the place with much clatter and yelling.

A little afterward a rather old Indian woman came out, and in front of us, for we were on horseback, nobody having dismounted. She began to dance along, making motions very indicative of pleasure, and at times stopping to talk to us, making signs with her hands as if bidding us welcome. After a short while I said to the commander that that was enough. So he gave presents of glass beads to all the women, they regaled us with their cacomites, and we said goodby to everybody in order to continue on our way. They were apparently sad because we were leaving, and I was moved to tenderness at seeing the joy with which we were welcomed by those poor Indians. Their color and other qualities of nakedness, slight beard, etc., are the same as those seen hitherto, and the same as those we saw farther on. Some wear the hair long, others short, and some have beards rather long and heavy.

Font and Anza had an excellent opportunity to observe aboriginal methods of navigation and fishing. At the western end of Carquinez Strait, says Anza (A, p. 140), five tule rafts crossed the strait in less than a quarter of an hour, the tide being slack. Font says, regarding these craft (F2, p. 320):

> We saw there some launches very well made of tule, with their prows or points somewhat elevated. They had been anchored near the shore with some stones for anchors, and in the middle of the water some Indians were fishing in one.... I saw that they were fishing with nets and that they anchored the launch with some very long slim poles.

These poles were measured and found to be about 13 varas long (roughly 35 ft.). Font goes on to describe the actual taking of fish:

> Among other fish which they caught the Indians who were fishing pulled out two very large ones, about two varas long, and their method of catching them was this: as soon as they felt from the pull made by the fish that it was in the net, which was tied to the two poles, they began gradually to raise one of the poles, and as soon as the fish and the net came in sight, without taking it from the water they gave the fish many blows on the head. Once I counted fifteen blows in succession and in another case twenty-odd. Now that it was dead and had lost its strength they took it from the net and put it inside the launch.

A soldier traded a piece of cloth for a fish. But the Indians

> ... before delivering it took the spawn from the stomach and an intestine like a pocket, and right there on the spot they ate the spawn raw and put what was left over in the intestine. They then went to eat the other fish, which they dispatched quickly. Making a little fire they put it in, and in a short time, almost before it was hot, like brutes they ate it as it was, almost raw.

Some war equipment was seen. Near the camp on Walnut Creek at Pacheco, the party was visited by local Indians with whom there was a little trouble.

> Some of them came to see us, carrying bows and arrows, for all had very good ones and well made, the bow of good wood, small and wound with tendons like those we saw on the Channel, and the arrows of little reeds, very smooth, well made, and with flints, transparent and very sharp. One came with a scalp hanging from a pole. This did not please me, for it suggested war.

Near the camp there were two villages: one, says Anza (A, p. 143), "which we left behind" and another, "which we have immediately ahead." Between the large rancheria of Tormey and the two just mentioned there appear to have been no Indian settlements whatever.

The day of Wednesday, April 3, was spent in crossing the low hills east of Concord and in traveling along the southern shore of Suisun Bay as far as Antioch Bridge. Neither Anza nor Font has particular comment concerning the one and one-half leagues, which brought them to the summit of Willow Pass, overlooking the area of Pittsburg. Beyond this point the explorers entered the northwest corner of the San Joaquin Valley, or the western tip of the delta. They probably had just left Costanoan territory, although, to be sure, the exact tribal boundaries are unknown. At any rate it is preferable to limit the present discussion to the region west and south of the low hills which extend from Port Chicago southeast to the vicinity of Byron. The rancherias which were seen near Antioch would therefore be more profitably considered in a survey of the valley tribes than in one of the East Bay and adjacent coast ranges.

Thursday, April 4, was spent in the famous attempt to cross the great tule swamps. In the course of this effort the party bore southeastward along the margin of the tules as far as the latitude of Bethany (Bolton, 1930, III: 148n). Thence they turned inland over Patterson Pass and, if Bolton's reconstruction is correct, followed up the ridge to the east of Arroyo Mocho. No trees or water were encountered until a point was reached not far southeast of Livermore. In the meantime, no Indians were seen and no traces of villages observed along the line of march.

The journey of Friday, April 5, took the party into the rough country due east of Mt. Hamilton as far as the southeastern edge of San Antonio Valley at the head of the east fork of Coyote Creek. The terrain was extremely hilly and was covered with oak and coniferous trees, probably principally digger pine, although Font says he saw "spruce." Great stretches of chamise (*Adenostema fasciculatum*), which Anza calls "Mattal," were observed. The descriptions make it clear that the type of vegetation and the general appearance of the country were essentially as they are today.

Only a few streams are mentioned: Arroyo Mocho is described merely as an "arroyo in a canyon." There were several small watercourses near the upper end of San Antonio Valley, and water in pools was found at the lower end near the night's camp. These streams may have been Sulphur Spring Creek and San Antonio Creek.

The area was destitute of natives. The only mention of Indians is by Font (F2, p. 414).

> In the course of the valley [San Antonio Valley] we saw some ruinous and abandoned little huts, but the only Indian seen was at a distance and running, for as soon as he saw us he fled for the brush of the Sierra like a deer.

Also, referring to the fruit of "a plant like a fig tree" which appears to be the buckeye, he says that "the heathen eat it, judging from the piles of its shells which we saw in the abandoned huts." A reasonable inference from Font's account is that in this area there were no permanent Indian settlements but in places there were temporary camp sites, used in the time of maturity of the local tree-crops (buckeye and perhaps acorns).

On April 6 and the first part of April 7 the party descended Coyote Creek, through Gilroy Hot Springs to the valley of the Pajaro River. The country throughout this stretch is described as hilly and rough, but little further description is given.

> In all this journey we did not see a single Indian, although we found some tracks of them, and in places a few signs and traces of ruined huts and small villages; for it is known that at times they go to the sierra and camp, especially during the seasons of the piñon and the acorn.

From the Font-Anza diaries, together with that of Crespi, certain tentative conclusions may be reached.

1. The distribution of vegetation in 1775 was substantially the same as described by the American settlers of 1850 and thereafter and, allowing for the devastating influence of the white man, more or less as it is today. The exceptions are the removal of forests, such as the redwood stand on

the Oakland hills, and the spread of introduced plants which has possibly occurred on the southern shore of Carquinez Strait. In the relatively untouched interior ranges there has been no significant alteration.

2. There is some question with regard to water supply. In his trip of 1772, between Milpitas and Pinole, Crespi mentions seeing or crossing 31 arroyos, all with running water. The date was from March 25 to 29. Anza and Font went at almost the same time of year (March 31-April 1, 1776) from Warm Springs to Rodeo, and report 20 or 21 arroyos. Of these only 2 or 3 contained abundant water; approximately 10 had only a small amount. The rest were either not described or were without water. Since there can have been no profound alteration in climate or geography in the few years between the two expeditions, the difference must be accounted for on the basis of relative precipitation during the preceding winters. Such a theory is supported by Font's statement (F2, p. 418) regarding the marshes and lagoons in Gilroy Valley: "Since it had not rained much this year it was quite dry...."

Examination of the modern maps is instructive. The U. S. Geological Survey quadrangles for the Bay Area were mapped in the decade 1895 to 1905, with subsequent re-editing. Thus the picture presented antedates the disruption of natural conditions caused by the population expansion of this century. The USGS sheets now show 20 streams between Milpitas and Rodeo which were named on the maps, or whose names are otherwise well recognized. These are, from south to north: Arroyo Coches Creek, Calera Creek, Scott Creek, Toroges Creek, Agua Fria Creek, Agua Caliente Creek, Mission Creek, Alameda Creek, San Lorenzo Creek, San Leandro Creek, the creek flowing past Mills College, the creek flowing out of Diamond Canyon through Fruitvale, Indian Gulch, Claremont Creek, Strawberry Creek, Codornices Creek, Wildcat Creek, San Pablo Creek, Pinole Creek, and Rodeo Creek. In addition there are approximately 12 unnamed creeks or arroyos descending the front slope of the hills onto the plain. The total, 32, conforms very closely with the descriptions left by the Spaniards in 1772 and 1776.

It is further to be noted that the government surveys of the period of 1900 showed all these streams as intermittent and therefore dependent for their flow upon the winter rainfall. Thus it is quite probable that in late March the amount of water might be copious (as in 1772) or relatively scanty (as in 1776). The conclusion seems warranted that, apart from dessication induced by such factors as soil damage, overgrazing, and diversion for minor irrigation projects, the local water supplies have not diminished since 1770. It then follows that under primitive conditions the natives had substantially the same quantity of water at their disposal as is available in the same area today.

3. The distribution of Indian population was quite clearly marked. Crespi (see above) encountered 5 villages from Milpitas to San Lorenzo. Anza mentions 6 villages in the same distance, most of which were north of Irvington. Both Crespi and Anza describe seeing no further villages until they reached Wildcat Creek. Thereafter they saw a village on each of San Pablo, Pinole, and Rodeo Creeks. Crespi puts 5 villages between Pinole and Crockett. Anza refers to only one, in addition to the one on Rodeo Creek, viz., the large village at Tormey. All accounts agree that there were no settlements between Crockett and Concord Valley, where 2 villages were found by both parties. On the return journey, Crespi traversed the valley from Walnut Creek to Dublin, Pleasanton, and near Niles, and noted a scattering of rancherias at least as far as Pleasanton. The Anza expedition, after leaving the delta, crossed the hills back of Mt. Hamilton and emerged near Gilroy, all without noting a permanent habitation site. From these accounts it is clear that the heavy concentration of population was along the Bay shore, locally centering on the large arroyos and avoiding the strip where Oakland and Berkeley now stand. Secondary centers were in the broader and lower interior valleys, west and north of Mt. Diablo. The narrow canyons and the brush-covered belts of the main axis of the Coast Range were destitute of inhabitants.

4. The numerical value of the population was estimated from the Crespi diary as 2,400. We may assay a comparable estimate from Font and Anza.

The six villages seen on the way from Warm Springs to San Lorenzo were largely abandoned by the inhabitants, who had fled in terror. Hence no population estimate is given. However an average of 100 persons each would be a reasonable assumption.

North of Berkeley an abandoned village was seen, probably on Wildcat Creek (possibly Strawberry Creek). Then a village of 100 persons was found on San Pablo Creek and another "fair sized" village probably on Pinole Creek. At Rodeo Creek was a village larger than the other two. Allowing 100 persons each for the abandoned village and the "fair sized" village and 150 for the one on Rodeo Creek, the four sites may be considered to represent at least 450 inhabitants. The village at Tormey had a population of 400, according to Font, and 500, according to Anza. No others are mentioned except the two in Concord Valley to which may be ascribed 100 persons each. If we use Font's estimate of 400 for the largest town, the total from

Warm Springs to Concord Valley is 1,650. This is reasonably close to the value of 1,900 derived from Crespi.

For the remainder of the Northern Costanoan territory, since Anza found no inhabitants south of the Livermore Valley, we have to use the figures derived from Crespi: approximately 500 for the interior valleys. The total, then is 2,150 as compared with the 2,400 based upon Crespi's account alone. In any case, the present estimate is purely tentative and must be considered in the light of the Mission baptism records which are subsequently described.

THE CAÑIZARES EXPEDITION

During the period of initial land exploration attempts were made to secure information by water. The most important such episode was the voyage, if one may call it that, made by José Cañizares in 1775. Cañizares was the first mate of the ship, San Carlos, under command of Juan Manuel Ayala. Ayala was commissioned to survey the entire San Francisco Bay area, but was unable to complete the task because of illness. He therefore delegated the interior exploration to Cañizares, who fulfilled the mission in late August and early September. The results of the trip are embodied, first, in a series of maps, and second, in a letter by Cañizares (1775) to Ayala. (For historical background, the work of Cutter, 1950, may be consulted.)

The maps are three in number, all versions of the same map drawn by Cañizares, and dated respectively 1775, 1776, and 1781. The first is very poorly executed and shows little more than the outline of the Bay; it is not reproduced here.

The second (map 2) is carefully done and gives an extensive list of localities. The original is in the Ministry of War, Madrid, Spain. It is an elaboration of, and a very great improvement on, a map drawn by Ayala in 1775 which showed merely the outline of San Francisco, without detail. Ayala's map has slight value, hence it is not shown here, but a copy is available in the Bancroft Library, Berkeley.

Since the present map is itself reproduced from a photograph of a photograph, the text of the legends in the boxes is very faint and blurred. To facilitate reading, these legends have been copied, with translations. The symbols used on the map are the Latin alphabet, using capitals, for twenty-three items; they then continue as Greek letters, which are difficult to decipher and do not run strictly in sequence. Hence, for convenience, I have substituted in the legends numbers for the Greek letters, number 1 following Z of the alphabetical series. The use of these numbers in conjunction with the Greek letters on the map will not be difficult. In the left-hand column is the Spanish text; in the right-hand column, a literal translation. No attempt is made to correlate the names given by Cañizares with those applied at the present time.

The third map (map 3) copies the second, is carefully done, and gives essentially the same information, but varies in minor points. Cañizares remained in San Blas for several years after his visit to San Francisco. During this period his 1776 map was apparently redrawn by Manuel Villavicencio, in 1781, presumably under the supervision of Cañizares himself. Whether it is more accurate than the 1776 map is open to question. Small and capital letters are used for the localities on the map and in the legends.

The letter describing the survey of the Bay was written by Cañizares and addressed to "Señor Capitan," obviously Ayala. It was dated September 7, 1775, "en este nuebo Puerto de S. Franco al abrigo de la Isla de Los Angeles." This document, which is an account of the first boat trip throughout San Francisco Bay, has never, to my knowledge, been published. Its intrinsic interest, consequently, as well as its bearing upon primitive geography and ethnography, warrants its presentation. A translation follows herewith. Various matters requiring comment are discussed immediately subsequent to the translation.

Cañizares' Report

On the four occasions when I went out to explore this port and survey its northeastern and north-northeastern portion I discovered what is shown on the map and is set forth here. To the north-northeast of the Island of Los Angeles, at a distance of one mile, there is a bay which runs north-northwest to south-southeast. The distance across between the points which form it is about two leagues and its length two and one-half. In its northwestern part there are three little islets, forming with the coast a narrow channel, which is shut off at its southwestern mouth by a shoal. Around all the margin of the bay are folded hills, with very few groves of trees and these which there are consist in part of laurel and live-oak; there may be seen in the interior to the west-northwest a forest of trees, which from afar seem to be pines. In the middle of this sound there is situated a great high cliff with some submerged rocks on the northeast side. As the map shows its depth is sufficient for anchorage; it no doubt is a roadstead for such vessels as have good cables and anchors, for much trouble would be caused by the current which flows here and which would not be less than four knots.

To the north-northeast of the said bay is a gap, the width of which might be two miles, in which are four white islands of small size, the northernmost forming with those on the southern shore a channel of 9 fathoms. These islands form the separation from another bay more capacious than the preceding, the diameter of which might be about eight leagues and the form of which is a perfect isosceles triangle. The above mentioned gap separates into two channels. The first, on the southwest shore, turns to the northwest a long mile distant, eventually disappearing in two big inlets, which are situated on the same shore, four leagues away from the opening which communicates with the first bay. If one goes a league and a half from the northwestern end of the inlet running farthest to the north, he rounds a point and discovers toward the west-northwest a spacious sound. I did not explore this because the channel which communicates with it is so restricted and narrow, there being scarcely three *codos* of water. From here a low island, level with the surface of the water, runs toward the east-northeast, ending at a point where the mountains divide. The second channel, which is quite large and capable of being sounded, immediately trends northeast, one quarter east, until it reaches the dividing point in the mountains where it enters a canyon, following the direction mentioned.

All this bay, which is called the round [bay]—although it is not such—is bordered by rough mountains without trees except two groves in the coves which are situated to the southwest. All the rest of it is arid, hilly and of melancholy aspect. Aside from these channels, in no part of the bay does its depth reach five *codos*; at low tide there are two and a half, and some areas are dry. It is not difficult to enter, but it will be difficult to get out of, for we found that the prevailing winds are from the southwest. Having examined its shores exhaustively, I found no fresh water, nor even indication that there had been any in former times.

Starting at the gorge which is at the northeastern end, the land forms a strait a mile and a half wide, clear, and capable of being sounded. At the eastern part of the entrance there is located a rancheria whose population might exceed 400 souls. I traded with these people, not to buy anything from them, but to present them with the beads which your Excellency has given me for this purpose, together with some of my used clothing. Contact with them was very useful to me and the crew on account of the many gifts they made us of very choice fish (among them salmon), seeds, and ground meal. After visiting them on four occasions I found them as they were the first time, and observed in them an urbane courtesy, and what is more, much modesty and neatness among the women. They tend to beg for nothing except for that which one gives them freely; without pressing to the limit of impertinence, like many others whom I have seen in this conquered territory. This rancheria has some rafts, better described as canoes, of tule rushes so carefully wrought and woven that it caused me admiration of their handiwork. In these they embark four men to go fishing, each one rowing with a double-ended oar. Using the latter they travel with such dexterity, as I found out, that they go faster than the launch. These were the first and the last Indians in this part of the north with whom I had communication.

Following the above mentioned channel, at a distance of a league from its mouth, the coast forms a cove so spacious, navigable, well provided with firewood and watering places, and protected from all winds that I judge it to be one of the best interior ports which our sovereign possesses, large enough to anchor a fleet of warships. I gave it the name of Port of the Assumption [Puerto de la Asumpta] on account of having reconnoitred it on the day of this festivity. To the southeast of this port the passage continues until it merges with the channel of the rancheria. Then it continues three leagues in an east-northeasterly direction. At the end of this distance it enters another bay with a depth of 13 fathoms, the latter diminishing until it reaches four. Into this bay flow several rivers, as is demonstrated by the fact that, leaving the salt water, one is able to drink fresh water from where the rivers come as if into a lake. One river comes from the east-northeast (this is the largest, the width of which will be about 250 varas), and the other, which is formed from quite small arms, flows from the northeast through a very low-lying region among swamps and sand dunes. Its depth does not reach two fathoms. These rivers have at their mouths some sand bars (as the commotion demonstrated to me) at a depth of half a fathom. The reason why I do not consider them navigable is principally that the second time I went to explore them I penetrated into the interior and ran aground both in the rivers and on the sand bars. In the bay into which these rivers discharge is another port more extensive than that of la Asumpta in which it is possible to moor any vessel whatever, but it would be difficult to get wood because of the remoteness of its shores. From the rancheria at the entrance which communicates with them, to the rivers themselves, all the coast of the east is covered with trees and all that on the west is arid, dry, full of locusts, and incapable of ever being populated.

The foregoing is what I discovered in this part of the north, and proceeding from the above-mentioned Island of Los Angeles the reconnoissance of the estuary to the southeast I describe as follows.

To the east of this island at a distance of two leagues there is another, rough, craggy, and of no value, which divides the mouth of the bay into two passages through which the sea penetrates about twelve leagues. The width in places is one, two and three leagues. The channel of this sound does not exceed four fathoms. Its width is adequate but on departing from it the distance of a pistol shot the depth does not reach two fathoms. The tip of this sound, which faces the east, forms, with a horseshoe-shaped headland, a pocket which, at low tide, is mostly dry. In this inlet are some logs to which are fastened black feathers, bunches of reeds and snail shells, which gave me the idea that they are fishing floats, since they are in the middle of the water. Beyond three leagues from the entrance of this estuary I estimate that nowhere is it possible to anchor, due to the lack of shelter. However, if such is the case, position ought to be maintained by force of cables because the same current is found here as in the northern part of the bay.

On the northeastern shore this bay is surrounded by high ranges of hills. At the mouth there is a luxuriant forest of live oak and another even larger at the upper end, together with a heavy growth of redwood. On the southwestern shore is a small estuary navigable only by small boats, and on the same shore two inlets in which anchorage is possible. Another, to the east, has a rancheria of Indians like those at Monterey. This coast appears to have locations very suitable for missions, although I examined them only from a distance.

All that is set forth in this account is what I have observed, witnessed, measured, and sounded during these days when, on orders from your Excellency, I went out to explore the interior of this port of San Francisco. For the record I am composing this account in this new port of San Francisco under the shelter of the Island of Los Angeles, today September 7, 1755.

It is clear that Cañizares, starting from what is now called Angel Island, crossed the Bay south of Point Richmond and proceeded northward between Point San Pablo and Point San Pedro into San Pablo Bay (Bahia de Guadelupe or Redonda). He explored Petaluma Creek (Estero de Nuestra Señora de la Merced) and the sloughs near Mare Island. Except for the southwest he found this bay surrounded by arid, treeless hills, thus agreeing with the opinion of the explorers by land. Just before entering Carquinez Strait, he saw a large rancheria. Although this village is not shown on the 1776 map it appears on the 1781 map at the southwest side of the western mouth of the strait. It is no doubt the same site described by Font.

One league, or perhaps three miles, from the entrance Cañizares encountered what he regarded as a spacious inlet or cove. Wagner (1937) and Cutter (1950) both state that this was Southampton Bay, opposite Port Costa (Puerto de la Asumpta). Cutter (p. 13) also claims that it has been filled with mud since 1775 and largely obliterated, but gives no evidence in support of the opinion. Cañizares describes Army Point, near Benicia (Puerto de los Evangelistas on the maps), and then gives an account of Suisun Bay which he says contained numerous islands filled with tules. Toward the upper end of these, on the maps, is shown fresh water. After attempting to penetrate the rivers, and running aground on sand bars, Cañizares returned to Angel Island before embarking for a reconnaissance of the southern area of the Bay. His description of the lower delta region is too confusing to be of value. He evidently did not fully understand the relations of the Sacramento and San Joaquin rivers at their junction.

Cutter (1950, p. 113) states, regarding vegetation, that Cañizares found the north shore of the Bay covered with trees and the south shore arid and dry. Cañizares says the vegetated shore was "east" and the arid shore was "west." Both maps depict trees on both shores, but with the heavier concentration on the south side. The 1781 map uses for "Bosques de buenas Maderas" the symbol "Q." The latter appears at the southeast end of San Francisco Bay, in the vicinity of Oakland and Alameda, on the south side of the rivers at the head of Suisun Bay, and on the north side, well above Suisun Bay. Small groups of trees appear on both maps at each entrance of

Carquinez Strait, in the vicinity of Pinole and of Martinez. There is no real evidence that there were trees on the north side of Carquinez Strait.

Although the data in the letter are scanty, the distribution of Indian population indicated by Crespi and Font is substantially confirmed. The text of the letter mentions only one rancheria, the one at or near Pinole or Selby, to which Cañizares (on the strength of four visits) ascribes a population of 400. This is the exact value given by Font, and seems to constitute very reliable evidence. Other villages are shown on the 1776 map, under the symbol "q." as "Rancherias de Indios Amigos," one on the north side of Southampton Bay, one near Martinez, one apparently near Bay Point (or Port Chicago), and one somewhere near Pittsburg. The same number of symbols (here "O") is shown on the 1781 map, but those on the south side of the strait are displaced several miles to the west. We can be reasonably sure therefore that Cañizares found four rancherias, including the one described in the letter, three on the south shore, one on the north. In view of the vague placement on the maps it is scarcely worth while to insist upon the precise location. As far as population is concerned, what information can be derived from Cañizares lends support to the conclusions based upon Crespi and Font.

EXPLORATORY AND PUNITIVE EXPEDITIONS, 1776-1811

After the return of Anza to Monterey in 1776 the San Francisco Presidio was founded. After this a joint expedition was sent out under José Joaquin Moraga and Francisco Quiros. The latter was to proceed by water and the former by land to a junction near the mouths of the rivers. The plan, however, miscarried, and Moraga went off on the earliest and the least known exploration of the main San Joaquin River. Meanwhile Quiros, with José Cañizares and Father Pedro Cambon, sailed up the Bay to a point quite close to that described by Cañizares in his first trip. The only account we have of this journey is contained in Palóu's New California (1926, IV: 127-130). No details of ecological interest are given and there is no mention of natives. For a detailed discussion of the exploration, reference may be made to Cutter (1950, pp. 24-26).

One further document requires mention at this point: The Historical, Political and Natural Description of California, by Pedro Fages, as translated by Herbert I. Priestley (1937). Written in 1775, this little volume has become a classic for its thorough and sympathetic description of the Indians of California by one who was in a position to write on the subject. Unfortunately, however, Fages discusses the Indians of the San Francisco Mission area and of the Central Valley of the interior, but he does not specifically refer to the natives of the East Bay. Hence his essay must be passed over with this brief citation.

Following the series of explorations which culminated in the Anza Expedition of 1776, little further official notice was taken of the East Bay counties until approximately 1794. There is an item in the Bancroft Library Transcript series (hereafter designated Bancroft Transcripts, or Bancroft Trans.), consisting of a letter from Fages to Moraga, January 23, 1783 (Prov. Rec., III: 83), noting that the latter had pursued the "indios gentiles Serranos" who had killed 18 head of livestock belonging to the Mission of San José. It is probable that many other unrecorded punitive expeditions were being undertaken throughout the two decades from 1775 to 1795.

In 1793 there was activity along the coast, in the course of which Lieutenant Francisco Eliza spent approximately two weeks exploring the Bay, but the documents available (Cutter, 1950, p. 29; Archivo General de la Nación, Mexico, Ramo Historia, Vol. 71, Expediente on Matute and the Bodega Settlement, and Account by Eliza, dated November 4, 1793, at San Blas) include no details of topography, vegetation, or ethnography worth recording.

Late in the following year, 1794, trouble began with the natives of the Contra Costa. The immediate cause appears to have been the zeal of the missionaries to push conversion in the area. On November 30, 1794, the military commander at San Francisco, Perez-Fernandez, wrote to Governor Borica (Bancroft Trans., Prov. St. Pap., XII: 29-30) that "the missionaries of San Francisco have requested an additional two or three men for the guard in order to go from Santa Clara to the other shore, in a northerly direction, as far as opposite the port [of San Francisco] to make conquests of the heathen...." The request was refused for reasons which in themselves throw light on the status of the East Bay natives:

> 1st. Because it is almost unknown country: there are indications that the heathen who occupy it are uncooperative.
>
> 2nd. He [the Commandant] does not believe that a priest, with two or three soldiers and some Christian Indians, constitutes a party sufficiently strong to cross and camp overnight in strange territory.
>
> 3rd. Although the Fathers believe this to be a favorable opportunity, because the heathen lack food, having lost their crop due to the severity of the drouth, and this will facilitate catching them, he does not have the means at his disposal for expeditions of this type.

Nevertheless, such forays were already in progress, for Perez-Fernandez reported that the Fathers at San Francisco "sent by sea to the islands and other shore opposite the mouth of the port some Mission Indians in rafts of tule on the 4th of this month to capture heathen." One of the rafts was carried as far out to sea as the Farallones, and two men were lost.

On March 3, 1795, Perez-Fernandez again wrote to Governor Borica from San Francisco (Bancroft Trans., Prov. St. Pap., XIII: 455-456.). (This, and many other letters cited here, are also to be found in the Archivo General de la Nación, Mexico City, Ramo Californias, Vol. 65, Expediente no. 3, entitled "Sobre la Muerte que dieron los Indios Gentiles a siete Indios cristianos de la Mission de San Franco.") He now announced the murder by the heathen of seven Christian Indians sent across the bay by Fray Antonio Danti to hunt for runaway neophytes. The culprits belonged to the rancheria of the

Chaclanes, and, says Perez-Fernandez, "these rancherias of the Chaclanes are in the country where the said Father Danti wanted to go, and whom I prevented from going, as I told your Excellency under date of November 29 last."

A lively correspondence ensued, reference to most of which may be omitted. An investigation was inaugurated and some type of scouting party was sent out. At least, we have record of a letter dated at Monterey, June 2, 1795, from Governor Borica to José Perez (Bancroft Trans., Prov. Rec., V: 56) in which the Governor orders Perez "to tell Sergeant Amador that he has received the report he sent concerning the reconnaissance to the Alameda, and that he shall continue this with the others who went with him." This is no doubt the expedition by Amador referred to by Danti in his diary (see below).

On June 23, 1795, from Monterey, Governor Borica rendered a full and final account of the affair to Viceroy Branciforte (Archivo General de la Nación, Californias, Vol. 65, Expediente no. 3, "Sobra la muerte ..." etc. Doc. no. 122, MS p. 79). Parts of this document are worth quoting. One of the survivors was a neophyte named Othon, whose story follows.

> Five old Christian Indians set out from the San Francisco Mission, including the alcaldes Pasqual and Rogerio, together with nine new Christians of the rancherias from the other shore of the bay, with orders from Father Missionary Fray Antonio Danti to bring back all the Christians who had run away. On the first day they crossed the bay in their boats and slept on the beach. On the second day at dawn they set out for the rancheria of the Chaclanes where they arrived at noon, and not having found any people in it, they kept on all that day and all night, travelling without sleep or rest, in spite of the rain, and reached the rancheria of the Chimenes at about two o'clock in the afternoon. They encountered there a great multitude, as many as there are in the mission [perhaps 900, according to Borica]. The men, armed with bows and arrows, came out of a big temascal with such a rush that they broke it to pieces, immediately beginning to shoot arrows, shouting, "Kill our enemies." The alcaldes, seeing this violence, tried to persuade the natives that we had not come to fight or to do harm, but the others took no heed and kept on shooting until they killed as many as seven....

Governor Borica goes on to say:

> This Othon and others told me that these Chimenes Indians
> are of a rough and valiant nature. They are at continual war
> with the neighboring villages, and particularly with the
> Tegunes. They live toward the north coast in the vicinity of
> the Port of Bodega. Their food is amole, bellota and pinole
> and their chiefs are called Mule and Yuma.

The identity of these Chimenes is something of a mystery. Certainly the Christian Indians, after leaving the rancheria of the Chaclanes (i.e., Saclanes), somewhere behind the Oakland hills, could not have even approached the port of Bodega, for they could not have crossed the Bay and the rivers on foot. Yet they traveled twenty-four hours, if Othon's account is even approximately correct. Hence they must have covered fully twenty-five or thirty miles, a distance which would have brought them to some point on the south shore of Carquinez Strait or Suisun Bay. If this is true, then they encountered representatives of the Huchiunes, the Karkines, or the Chupunes, the only tribal groups known definitely to have inhabited the area. The statements of Othon, as transmitted by the Governor, regarding the number of Chimenes, as well as their ferocity, must be heavily discounted (although the smashing of the temescal is a touch which would hardly be supplied by imagination alone). One hundred, or even fifty, infuriated warriors would no doubt have appeared to be thousands to the fourteen terrified Christians, and the Governor would hardly want to report to the viceroy that his Mission Indians had been routed by a handful of wild natives. On the other hand, the incident proves the existence of a sizable rancheria somewhere in northern Contra Costa County in 1795.

FR. ANTONIO DANTI'S EXPEDITION

In the late fall of the year 1795, following the reconnaissance of Sergeant Amador, of which no written record survives, another and more pretentious expedition covered the lower east side of San Francisco Bay. There are two accounts available describing this trip. One was written by Hermenegildo Sal (1795), a soldier from Monterey, and the other by Fray Antonio Danti (1795). The two documents are very similar in form and give indication of collaboration in the writing. Sal's "Informe" is the longer and the more circumstantial but is so badly executed as to be nearly incomprehensible in some of its passages. Danti's "Diario" is very succinct but clearly written. Since both accounts cover the same events, only one needs to be presented in full. Here follows the "Diario" of Danti, commencing with line 5, page 196 of the Bancroft Transcript.

22 October: After lunch we set out [from Santa Clara] for the place called the Alameda. We arrived by nightfall at the first arroyo, which is [the one mentioned by] Sergeant Amador. At sunrise of the 23rd we went on our way upstream, as far as we could go on horseback, which will be about one league distant from the camping place. We wanted to examine the origin of the stream but the soldier told us that it emerged opposite the town. When the various sections of the arroyo had been explored, the water was found to be of the same quantity throughout and in my opinion can irrigate two or three ditches of corn at the same time because of the slope of the land. The removal of the water is not a great problem, for the heathen took it out in two distinct places. There is much fine land and easily worked. The timber in this place is scarce, as is also the firewood. It is to the north of Santa Clara about 6 or 7 leagues. In this arroyo are three empty houses.

Having examined all that has been described, we went along the foot of the hills. We encountered [p. 197] another watercourse which was dry, and where there is the stone called cantarra [a type of clay]. This is not far from the camping place. A little farther on is the lime pit, which is no more than caliche [crude, soft limestone]. We arrived at the Alameda, but before reaching it there are three little creeks, one of which could irrigate a garden. The other two, if widened, could serve as watering places for cattle. We went on to the river of the Alameda, which is filled with many large boulders from floods and is heavily overgrown with willow, cottonwood, and some laurel. Where the water runs, the stream is half a vara deep and 4 varas across, and in other places it widens and contains more water. We proceeded along it with much effort for about a league and a half, at which point it is joined by another arroyo from the north, the main stream continuing on to the east. We examined the feasibility of removing water and found it to be not impossible but very difficult. This is because of the gravelly nature of the soil and because several ditches would have to be constructed to regulate the floods, and in case these occurred annually a dam would have to be built. Following the arroyo farther down, we saw where the water disappears, perhaps a quarter of a league from the hills. At a distance of a league the water comes out again. In all this stretch [p. 198] the bed of the river, or arroyo, is deep and the removal of water impossible. In this locality the arroyo is covered with a dense stand of woods: cottonwoods and willows. A short section through which the river flows is reached by the tides of the bay.

24th day: We left for the north, staying close to the hills. There are very fine plains and very good pasturage. We encountered several water holes where cattle might drink.

From the Alameda, which is called San Clemente, to the first arroyo northward, which is called San Juan de la Cruz, the distance is about three leagues. The latter creek has little water and a few cottonwoods. We followed along the hills until the Mission of Our Father San Francisco came into view. At this point we turned around; the plains run to the parallel of the presidio. After eating, we surveyed the shore of the bay where, after about a league with no water, we came upon some salt marshes which without doubt are those which Sergeant Amador mentions in his diary. At the present time they do not contain salt, from which I infer that they are marshes like those of San Mateo where in dry years the salt crystallizes out.

25th day: We returned [p. 119] to the first watering place, called San Francisco Solano, at which it is possible to establish the mission, although there is likely to be much damage inflicted by the horses of the town. A cross was placed on a small hill, for in all the region we covered there is no place more suitable. The unconverted heathen are fairly numerous, according to the many trails which are to be seen. In the same plain there are three moderate-sized rancherias.

The above is what I consider adequate for the information of your reverence. If anything be lacking you will advise me so that your reverence may form an appropriate opinion.

The itinerary may be followed with reasonable precision. The journey of the 22nd brought the party to a creek 6 or 7 leagues (Sal says 6) north of Santa Clara. Taking the league as 2.7 miles, this distance puts them on Mission Creek not far from Mission San José (called by Danti, San Francisco Solano). On the morning of the 23rd they penetrated to the headwaters of this creek, approximately 2 or 3 miles into the hills. The idea that this creek came out opposite the town of San José is manifestly an error.

Returning to the starting point and then going along the foot of the hills for 2 leagues, as Sal says in the "Informe," they reached Alameda Creek very close to Niles. They then went upstream to the junction of Stonybrook Creek in the hills and then retraced their steps to Niles. The water disappeared just southwest of the town (1/4 league from the hills) and reappeared one league below, perhaps a mile southwest of Decoto and 3 miles east of Alvarado and on the edge of the salt marshes.

On the 24th the party proceeded 3 leagues northward to the stream called San Juan de la Cruz. From the distances, this can have been no other than San Lorenzo Creek. If so, they went on out to the shore of the Bay and saw San Francisco from a point just west of San Lorenzo. A few miles now to the southward would have brought them to the salt marshes just southwest of Mt. Eden. The hills they ascended were the Coyote Hills near Newark. From this point they crossed the plain directly to Mission San José and thence to Santa Clara.

Danti notes on Mission Creek the presence of three empty houses, indicating at least transient occupation by a few natives. Toward the end of the "Diario" he says that the unconverted heathen are "fairly numerous" and that on the plain there are three "moderate-sized" rancherias. Actually, therefore, he saw no indigenous heathen, and could find traces of no more than would inhabit three rancherias of dubious size. It will be remembered that Crespi reported in 1772 that there were five villages between Milpitas and San Lorenzo, whereas Anza in 1776 found six. Danti, in a much more exhaustive survey, located only three. It is evident that during the intervening twenty years the native population in southwestern Alameda County had been seriously depleted, reduced perhaps more than half. Accordingly it must be recognized that the documents relating to the Danti-Sal expedition (and all later ones) are of little value for estimating the preconquest population of the East Bay. The reduction was due, of course, to conversion by the missions and disturbance of the native economy, as well as to introduced diseases.

RAYMUNDO EL CALIFORNIO'S TRIP

Activity along the Contra Costa was again intensified in 1797. This time, as in 1795, the reason for attention in the official records was a minor expedition which got into trouble. Reference to the purely routine correspondence is here omitted and citation is made only of those letters containing matter of intrinsic interest.

On June 20, 1797, the commandant, José Arguello, wrote from San Francisco to the missionaries at San José (Bancroft Trans., Prov. St. Pap., XV: 213). He had just learned that a Christian Indian, named Raymundo el Californio, had left the mission at the head of about 30 or 40 other Indians in pursuit of fugitive Christians on the other shore. He asked for confirmation of this report. Within a few days he had his answer. In an undated letter, probably subsequent to June 22, from San Francisco he informed Governor Borica what had happened (Bancroft Trans., Prov. St. Pap., XV: 216-217).

> The Indians under Raymundo el Californio returned, completely dispersed because the winds and high waves swamped many of them. Since they did not tell the same story, he [Arguello] questioned Raymundo, who declared: having reached the other shore he found in three rancherias of the Cuchillones several Christians, men, women and children. On retreating to the beach with them, he was attacked by the other Indians of the place, but he succeeded in embarking in the boats without their having started a battle. Two of his group who had lagged behind were pursued by the Indians and were forced to jump into the water. Soon they were rescued by a boat, one of them having received a spear wound in the head, but of little severity. While they [the whole party] were all retiring, a storm came up which dispersed them widely. When they tried to follow Raymundo, they were twice forced back to the territory of the Cuchillones. Seeing that their boats were being broken up and thinking themselves lost, they abandoned the boats and went by land, without leaving the edge of the beach until they arrived opposite San Francisco, where they came upon a rancheria of heathen, named Santa Anna. The inhabitants made them welcome and furnished them with tules from their own houses, with which they constructed other boats and crossed to this shore.

The expedition sailed across, apparently to the region of Richmond or San Pablo. Later, the fugitives followed the beach to the vicinity of Oakland and San Leandro. The existence of a rancheria of heathen, bearing the name of Santa Anna, is peculiar. The name was familiarly applied without church sanction, or it was a village containing Christian converts rather than heathen. In either event, complete absorption of the natives into the Spanish Colonial system as far north as Oakland is implied. Also noteworthy is the casual manner in which the Mission Indians crossed and recrossed the Bay at its widest point in tule rafts.

PEDRO AMADOR'S EXPEDITIONS

On July 8, Sergeant Pedro Amador reported from San José to the Governor (Bancroft Trans., Prov. St. Pap., XV: 371-373) that two heathen, or wild, Indians were trying to stir up a revolt among the Christians of San José. "These two Gentiles are from the rancherias of the Sacalanes, from those which committed the offenses against the Christians of San Francisco. All of them are neighbors of those of the valley of San José in that part of the shore opposite San Francisco." Since the Valley of San José was the valley of upper Alameda Creek, extending from Sunol to above Pleasanton, this statement tends to place the Sacalanes in the general area west of Livermore and in the hills to the northward.

Two days later, July 10, the Governor answered Amador's letter, from Monterey (Bancroft Trans., Prov. St. Pap., XVI: 71-72), ordering him to go with two soldiers and twenty civilians to the rancheria of the Sacalanes and capture both the chiefs and all fugitive Christians. Amador carried out the order immediately and, after his return, submitted a report to the Governor in the form of a diary, together with a letter, both dated July 19 at San José. The diary in full is to be found in the Archivo General de la Nación, Ramo Californias, Vol. 65, Doc. no. 1, MS p. 93. The essential portions are worth reproducing and are translated as follows.

Amador's Diary (1797)

[July 6 to 12 inclusive were spent making preparations.]

July 13. We set forth [from Mission San José] on the campaign in the evening. I traveled all that night till dawn and hid with the party in a brushy ravine throughout the day,

July 14. In the evening we arrived at the place where the rancheria of the Sacalanes was located.

July 15. At dawn we attacked the said rancheria. We met much resistance from the Indians in it. Although we repeatedly told them that we did not wish to fight but only to take away the Christians, they admitted to no persuasion but began to shoot so as to kill one of our horses and wound two others. Seeing this opposition, we used our weapons in order to subdue them so that they would surrender. Some were killed, for they refused for two hours to give up. Finally, it was necessary to dismount and throw them back with swords and lances, for they have some wells in the middle of the village which are like walls and which can be strongly defended. There may have been about fifty persons, men and women.

There were three rancherias close together, and with the destruction of this one, the inhabitants of the others fled. We captured only two from the second rancheria, although in the first the number captured was thirty, including both Gentiles and Christians. Having carried out an investigation and having ascertained the guilty ones and the Christians, I made it clear to the rest, through interpreters, that we did not wish to do them any harm. They said they wanted to obey and that they well understood that we had no evil intentions. I liberated the Gentiles and we set forth toward the region of the Juchillones.

We had gone but a short distance when there began to assemble a great many Indians, uttering shrieks and cries, so that we had to go into line of battle again. Falling upon them, we killed one, and with this they all retreated. We followed our course in the direction we were going and concealed ourselves in a ravine near the beach. It has much timber, water, and firewood, good for a settlement. There we spent all the day hidden until nightfall when we went on to the rancheria of the Juchillones.

At dawn [of July 16] we reached the place where were gathered all the Christians whom we wanted, together with those Gentiles who had participated in the attempt to kill Raymundo and his people. We struck the first, second, and third village in the same morning. When we reconnoitred the Indians of the last rancheria, which is very large, the inhabitants were just about to open hostilities, but being admonished by the interpreters that we had not come to harm them but to hunt for Christians, they were pacified. We pointed out to them that we had punished the others because they had fought with us. Then we returned to the first village with the Christians and Gentiles and there assembled all those who had been concealed in the three rancherias. Having separated out all those we had caught and were taking with us, we set forth on our return journey. The Gentiles had been cautioned, the same as the preceding ones, that we did not wish to injure them if they did not harm us. We followed our course of retirement along the

coast. We reached an arroyo with little water and much
timber, in which we passed the night with sentinels in the
camp and at two advanced posts.

July 17. At night we reached an arroyo which has much
water, much timber and firewood, and also has nearby
redwood, and very much good sand and some very long
valleys.

July 18. We reached Mission San José at a distance of six
leagues.

Amador's diary helps us to estimate the location and numbers of the tribal
groups in question. After leaving Mission San José in the evening, his party
traveled till dawn. Since all the men were mounted, this means a probable
rate of 4 miles an hour for at least six hours, or 24 miles. The following day,
"in the evening," they reached the first rancheria of the Sacalanes. Allowing
a ride of three hours, the total distance would be 36 miles. Since there is no
mention of the coast, the route must have been the well-known inland trail
through Pleasanton and Dublin. Hence the destination was in the Walnut
Creek-Lafayette area. This effectually disposes, I think, of any possibility
that the Sacalanes could have inhabited the Livermore Valley.

Further evidence is provided by subsequent events. After spending
presumably several hours subduing the Sacalanes, Amador went over near
the beach where he spent "all day," obviously meaning the rest of the day.
Probably no more than three or four hours were consumed in the actual
ride, or a distance of 9 to 12 miles. It must be remembered that now Amador
was burdened with captives, who traveled on foot at a likely rate of no more
than 3 miles per hour. Hence he must have reached the bay shore in the
vicinity of Richmond.

At nightfall, the party went on to the rancheria of the Juchillones, which
may have been a few miles up the coast. No indication is given of distance,
except that at dawn they reached their destination. The most probable guess
is that the rancheria was somewhere on the southeast shore of San Pablo
Bay between Pinole and Rodeo. This view is supported by the account of
the return trip.

After having attacked three rancherias, conducted negotiations,
identified and secured several dozen captives, Amador began his retreat
"along the coast." At night they reached a well watered arroyo, which could
have been San Pablo Creek or Wildcat Creek. On the 17th the party spent
the whole day moving down the shore to an arroyo, near some redwoods,
which, according to the notation of the following day, was 6 leagues

from Mission San José. The arroyo which best fits the description and the distance (about 15 mi.) is San Leandro Creek. This, in turn, is just about a day's journey from San Pablo Creek for a military party encumbered with numerous prisoners. There are therefore reasonable grounds contained in Amador's diary for placing the Juchillones on the shore of San Pablo Bay from Point San Pablo northeast to Rodeo or beyond.

With respect to numbers, it may first be noted that Amador found three rancherias fairly close together for each tribal group: Sacalanes and Juchillones. The only indication of size for the Sacalanes is the mention of 50 men and women who participated in the defense of the first rancheria; The other two rancherias had been deserted. Perhaps a maximum of 300 and a minimum of 100 inhabitants for all three villages is indicated. For the Juchillones, Amador states only that the third rancheria was "very large." This may be taken to mean a population of over 100, and on this assumption the total might be set within the range suggested for the Sacalanes, i.e., 100-300.

In the letter to the Governor covering his report, dated July 19 at Mission San José (Bancroft Trans., Prov. St. Pap., XV: 319-320) Amador says, regarding the Cuchillones [Juchillones] "... it is certain that there are many rancherias and very big ones; and this is the reason why they assemble to hold their councils and eat many seeds." This statement would favor a fairly large population. Furthermore, in replying to Amador on July 21, Governor Borica (Bancroft Trans., Prov. Rec., V: 118) notes that the expedition brought back 83 Christians and 9 Gentiles. This fact shows that the two tribal groups, Sacalanes and Juchillones, had already been able to absorb the losses occasioned by the missionization of 40 persons per tribe—plus the conversion of probably many others who were not fugitives or at least were not captured by Amador, plus the attrition due to disease and disruption of food supplies—and yet were in a position to maintain a total of 6 rancherias, each of moderate to large size. The preconquest population per group must have reached at least 300 and very likely was much greater.

After Amador's return in late July a full-scale investigation was ordered. A great many Indians were interrogated in an effort to discover the cause, not only of the bitter hostility of the East Bay villages, but also of the incorrigible fugitivism which plagued the local missions. Two sets of testimony are on record (Archivo General de la Nación, Ramo Californias, Vol. 65, no. 3, MS p. 101, and no. 5, MS p. 109, dated respectively August 9 and September 16, 1797) which are of interest to the student of Indian psychology but of no particular ethnographic significance.

Meanwhile, more small expeditions were sent out. The records of the pueblo of San José (Bancroft Trans., Dep. St. Pap., San José, I: 81-82) show that on July 2 an expedition was ordered to capture and punish Gentiles who had killed two mares. Later reports indicated that this objective had been accomplished. Subsequently, in a letter to Governor Borica dated at San José on September 3, Sergeant Amador described another expedition (Bancroft Trans., Prov. St. Pap., XV: 317-318). He says that "he set out at 8:00 p.m. on August 26 in search of the rancheria Pijugma. First they went to that of Juquili and at dawn fell upon the first rancheria [presumably Pijugma] where they did not find the chieftain they sought." However, they afterwards caught this chief, with three others, all of whom they took to the mission. Amador says the rancherias "will be about 10 leagues from the mission and are opposite the beach." The latter statement, together with the fact that the distance was covered in one night's travel on horseback, suggests the area of the Livermore Valley.

The Sacalanes and Cuchillones appear again in a letter from Governor Borica to the Viceroy, dated at Monterey, March 14, 1799 (Bancroft Trans., Prov. Rec., VI: 443-444). The transcript reads:

> Says that only in serious cases should vigorous measures be taken against them [Indians]. The Indians fugitive from the Mission of San Francisco, Sacalanes and Cuchillones, are being recovered by means of emissaries and parties of soldiers who are treating them with the greatest gentleness and humanity. In the month of June, last, 18 of all ages and sexes came back to their ministers. In the following December the corporal of the guard of San José brought in 33 who wished to remain there [Mission San José], as they had agreed with the Father President, because of the horror with which they regard the Mission of San Francisco.

A year later there was another attack on these unfortunate people. In a letter dated at San Francisco, May 20, 1800, the commander, Arguello, wrote to Governor Arrillaga (Bancroft Trans., Prov. St. Pap., XVIII: 32-33) that, in conformity with orders to investigate the murder of two Christian Indians at Mission San José, Sergeant Amador went out with a large party to the "sierra." In another letter of Alberni to Governor Arrillaga, Monterey, July 2, 1800 (Bancroft Trans., Prov. St. Pap., XVIII: 33-34), the people concerned are described as "the Gentiles of San José called Sacalanes, who were committing depredations." Amador's own account, dated May 14, 1800, at San Francisco, is contained in another transcript (Bancroft Trans., Prov. St. Pap., Ben. Mil., XXVIII: 130-132). It reads thus:

Left Santa Clara on the 7th—arrived at the location of the rancheria he sought. It was not there—it had been moved. On the 9th they found it. The Indians fled to the sierra from which they threatened, but did not attack. With the best horses a few of the warriors were caught. To hold on to them sword and lance had to be employed and a captain was killed. Then the expedition retired from the rancheria, and waited about three hours to be sure that the Indians were not going to attack, for it was not easy to reach the spot where they were.

The expedition descended to the plains of San José [probably the western end of the Livermore Valley], where it awaited the corporal and four soldiers sent to take the 10 captive Indians to the garrison at San José.

At 3:00 p.m. on the 10th the corporal and four men returned. They traveled all night to reach the rancherias.

The 11th he fell upon the seven rancherias to gather up the 21 Christians who were delivered by the chiefs. None of the Gentiles wanted to be made a Christian. In two of the rancherias the Gentiles almost took up arms.... The 12th the expedition arrived at Mission San José....

Since no specific information is given, it may be assumed that this expedition penetrated the area lying between Mt. Diablo and the Livermore Valley, perhaps getting as far north as Walnut Creek. It is stated and implied that the Sacalanes were in a condition of great disorganization. They had been driven into the hills, apparently widely scattered and probably seriously depleted in numbers.

LUÍS PERALTA'S EXPEDITIONS

The last information we possess concerning this group of natives comes from the year 1804. In 1803, a letter, dated May 11 at Loreto, from Governor Arrillaga to the Viceroy (Archivo General de la Nación, Ramo Californias, Vol. 9, MS p. 433) mentions the fact that 20 Christians, sent out by the missionaries of Santa Clara, were attacked and routed by Gentiles who killed their "principal." In connection with this murder, and with a supposed plot to destroy Mission San José, the testimony of witnesses was taken a year later (Archivo General de la Nación, Ramo Californias, Vol. 9, MS pp. 437-439, June 21, 1804, San José, Luís Peralta in charge). On September 27, 1804, from Santa Clara, in a letter to an unnamed captain,

Luís Peralta (Bancroft Trans., Prov. St. Pap., XVIII: 334) advised that the expedition he made against Gentile Indians had no satisfactory results, because of lack of guides. On September 29, Arguello, at San Francisco, wrote to Governor Arrillaga (Bancroft Trans., Prov. St. Pap., XVII: 354) that he had ordered Peralta to go to the "Sierra de San José" in pursuit of Gentile assassins of Christians, but Peralta could not catch them.

Peralta went out a second time. Arguello, from San Francisco, on October 26, wrote again to Governor Arrillaga (Bancroft Trans., Prov. St. Pap., XVII, 358-359) that Peralta could not catch the killers of the Mission Indian Jorge, but he did catch 11 Christians, and after leaving the women and children at the mission, brought 32 "gandules" ("rogues," "rascals," a colloquial term for renegade Indians) to the Presidio. Since the "Sierra de San José" was the coast range behind the East Bay it is clear that the remnant of the people who originally inhabited the interior had taken to the hills in a last stand against the invader. After 1804 all mention of them ceases.

The Cuevas Affair. —In 1805 occurred what is called the "Cuevas Affair." This event has significance for the Alameda and Contra Costa natives, rather than those of the delta or lower San Joaquin Valley, only if the Indians concerned were bona fide aboriginal inhabitants of the inner coast ranges, as Cutter (1950) seems to assume. We must therefore review the evidence.

On January 16, 1805, José Antonio Sanchez wrote from San José to José Arguello (Bancroft Trans., Prov. St. Pap., XIX: 34-35) that Father Pedro Cuevas had asked for a guard to visit and confess invalids in a "rancheria of Christian Indians." The guard was granted. When the party arrived at the designated rancheria, they did not find the invalids. Whereupon they continued farther to another rancheria, where they were attacked and badly mauled. The most reliable account is probably that of Governor Arrillaga, contained in a letter dated March 11, 1805, at Loreto, to the Viceroy (Archivo General de la Nación, Ramo Californias, Vol. 9, MS pp. 452-453). According to him, Father Cuevas was intending to confess Indians at a "nearby" rancheria called Asiremes. José Arguello (January 31, 1805, San Francisco, letter to Governor Arrillaga, Bancroft Trans., Prov. St. Pap., XIX: 36-37) calls it Asirenes and says it was in the "interior of the Sierra." No other mention of this rancheria occurs, to my knowledge, in the contemporary documents.

The Governor then recounts the casualties: the major domo and two Mission Indians killed, Father Cuevas and two Indians wounded, all the horses killed. He adds that Sergeant Luís Peralta immediately went out with a punitive expedition.

Peralta's story is told in a diary dated January 30, at San Francisco (Bancroft Trans., Prov. St. Pap., XIX: 33-34). He left San Francisco January

19 for Santa Clara to raise personnel. With 18 soldiers and some civilians he arrived on the 22nd "at the point where the evil doers made their attack." They found the body of the major domo, and "since, due to the rain, they could find no trace of the Indians, they camped in the Sierra." Very clearly there was no rancheria or other habitation at this point.

Peralta continues that he found two Gentiles who told them where the rancheria was. Early on January 23 they marched to the place designated. When the occupants began hostilities, the Spaniards fell upon them and killed five. The remainder "fired at us from some barrancas, part of them from a wood [*bosque*] which was located there. Soon all retreated to the wood." The whites then attacked the wood and cleared it out, capturing 25 persons, all women and children, and killing another five "Indios." At dark they retired for the night "to where the horses had been left," but the following day returned briefly to the wood, where they found no one. Then all hands returned to the mission.

Despite the fact that at least 40 Indians were encountered, there is no indication in the Peralta diary of any permanent habitation. The attack on Father Cuevas occurred at a point where no trace of natives could be found. The battle in which Peralta was engaged took place among barrancas and in a forested area—again, no suggestion of houses or of even a temporary settlement.

With regard to the name of the tribal group concerned there seems to be no question. In a letter of May 30, 1805, from San Francisco to Governor Arrillaga (Bancroft Trans., Prov. St. Pap., XIX: 42) José Arguello speaks of "the rancheria of the Luechas, where the attack against Father Cuevas took place." Much later, José Maria Amador, writing for H. H. Bancroft in 1877 (Bancroft Manuscript, Amador, Memorias, translated by Earl R. Hewitt), referred to "Cuevas, who was going to instruct in the Christian faith the heathen at the Lochis rancheria...." Here is a discrepancy, for the contemporary documents state that Father Cuevas intended to exercise his religious functions at the rancheria of the Asirenes. However, it is clear enough that the outrage itself was perpetrated by the Luechas.

The location of the people—wholly apart from the question of where the attack occurred—is equivocal. That the attack took place in the Sierra is beyond doubt, but that the home of the offenders was likewise in the hills is not so sure. Cutter (1950, p. 92) relies upon a statement of Amador (below) when he states: "The Indians had turned out to be the Luechas, residents of the hills between Livermore and the San Joaquin Valley"; and "this would place them at the foothills east of Mount Diablo at the entrance of the Valley." The pertinent sentence in Amador's Memorias (MS, p. 13) reads thus: "rancheria de Loechas, como 14 leguas al oriente de la mision, arriba del actual pueblo de Livermore a 4 o 5 leguas de dist a ."

Allowing, conservatively, 2.5 miles per league, the total distance from the mission, if Amador is correct, would be 35 miles. The rancheria would be from 10 to 12.5 miles from Livermore. The term "above" ("arriba de....") does not necessarily mean toward the geographical north, but the direction may be taken as in the quadrant from north to east. The arc of the circumference of a circle with center at Livermore and radius of 12 miles passes approximately from San Ramon in the northwest, well south of Mount Diablo, across the very rough lower spurs of the mountain massif to the mouth of Kellogg Creek near Byron to the northeast. From here it runs along beyond Altamont, close to Mountain House and Midway, as far as upper Corral Hollow to the southeast. This entire stretch is devoid of any indication of substantial aboriginal occupancy, either in the eighteenth-century documents or in modern archaeological research.

Let us also note Amador's total: 14 leagues east of the Mission, or fully 35 miles. The horseback trail of 1805 followed pretty much the shortest highways of today: from Mission San José to Sunol and thence to Livermore via Pleasanton or directly across the low hills east of Sunol. By the first route the distance is 18 miles, by the second 16 miles. Using the larger value, 18 miles, the rancheria would have been not 12, but 17 miles beyond Livermore, which would have put it definitely in, or on the edge of, the San Joaquin Valley.

This conclusion agrees with Cutter's, referred to above, with respect to the location of the attack, but the theory that these Luechas actually were "residents" of the inner coast ranges and hence to be included in the area here being considered is contradicted by the following points.

1. As indicated above, no contemporary account explicitly states that an inhabited village was encountered or entered by the Californians during the Cuevas campaign.

2. There is no other documentary evidence for villages actually in the hills due west of the San Joaquin Valley floor.

3. In a letter to Governor Arrillaga dated February 28 at San Francisco (Bancroft Trans., Prov. St. Pap., XIX: 39-40), José Arguello mentions a second expedition by Sergeant Peralta "to the sierra where the Indians were who attacked Father Cuevas." In the course of this journey by Peralta: "A chief of the big rancheria on the river San Francisco, called Pescadero, came to give Sergeant Peralta the assurance that neither he nor his people had taken part in the attack against Father Cuevas and his guard." Since Pescadero was the main rancheria of the Bolbones, near Bethany, and since the latter

were a delta tribe of either Miwok or Yokuts stock, it is unlikely that the chief would have feared a confusion of identity with a tribal group which was indigenous to the hill country to the west. But if the guilty parties were plains or delta people, he might well have been apprehensive.

4. Amador, in the Memorias (MS, pp. 14-15) says that "Lieutenant Gabriel Moraga and his troops set out to punish the evildoers. The latter had already moved to the San Joaquin River and gone to a rancheria called Pitenis." Pitenis was on the main San Joaquin River above Lathrop.

Here again we see an affinity of the Luechas with the Valley, rather than the hill habitat, for the refugees, if traditionally and aboriginally sierran, would have been very unlikely to seek sanctuary in the depths of the Valley.

5. Schenck (1926) has no hesitation in placing the Luechas (or Leuchas) in approximately the region of Manteca and says Pitenis was one of their villages.

On the whole, the writer feels that the evidence is insufficient to warrant placing the Luechas in the coast ranges as a group aboriginally native to that area. They are preferably to be regarded as a valley people, of unknown ethnic affiliation, who penetrated the hills from the east and for some reason got into difficulty with Father Cuevas and his followers. At all events they cannot be considered Costanoans.

FR. JOSÉ VIADER'S FIRST EXPEDITION

In the years following the Cuevas episode numerous expeditions were sent out which opened up the interior of California. Most of these are more appropriate to a consideration of the interior valleys than to a survey of the coast ranges to the east of San Francisco Bay. Two, however, contain sufficient pertinent material to warrant their citation. They are the first expeditions by Father Fray José Viader in 1810 and that by Father Fray Ramón Abella in 1811. Both these missionaries explored the delta region and the rivers but on their way to the valley they passed through the East Bay and left descriptions of considerable interest. A translation of this portion of the diaries is presented without comment and a discussion of the native tribes mentioned is deferred until a subsequent section.

Fr. José Viader's Diary (1810)

August 15. [Left San José Mission and went 6 leagues north to the valley of San José.]

August 16. In this day, following the same direction, north, we traveled about 6 leagues before noon, and having killed two bears and a very large deer, we stopped to rest at the headwaters of a stream called Walnut Creek. This stream, although it has good water, is running very little. In the afternoon, in the same direction, having traveled another six leagues, having killed a deer and an antelope, and having observed fine country well covered with trees, all without water, we arrived at dark at the end of Walnut Creek. This is at the beginning of some inlets on the northeast side of a well known plain, well covered with trees (among others large walnuts).

August 17. We passed this day (without moving camp) in scouting the plain and adjacent hills, the lands of which belong to the Tarquines, most, or almost all, of whom are Christians of San Francisco. We have seen the mouth of the two rivers, one of which comes from the north and the other from the southeast. Uniting, they enter one of the estuaries which reach from San Francisco. In all this region, very well known for its climate, fine lands, much wood and walnut groves, the only water we found was one pool of stagnant water, another with good water although its water could not escape, and a spring which flows a little and which is next to the willow grove close to the inlet where it is said used to be the rancheria of the Tarquines. Granting what has been said and that Walnut Creek contains very little water, the area seems to me unsuitable for a foundation. In all this day we killed three bears and 11 deer....

August 18. We set out early from the above mentioned place, and going to the east we crossed the main range and in 7 leagues reached the San Joaquin, or, as they say, the Tulare River. This is one-quarter of a league wide and appears to be very deep and to feel the tides of the sea. Here we stopped to rest between the river and a very large oak forest. This is said to be the land of the Tulpunes. We saw neither them nor any sign or trace of heathen.... In the afternoon we went two leagues further, toward the east, in the middle of the oak forest ... and this place also belongs to the Tulpunes, who did not let themselves be seen.

August 19. [Went on southeast to Pescadero.]

FR. RAMÓN ABELLA'S EXPEDITION

Abella's Diary (1811)

October 15. At 10 o'clock in the morning we left the embarcadero at the port and stopped at the Island of Los Angeles because the tide was changing. At about 4 o'clock in the afternoon when the tide was favorable we set out and arrived at the point of the Huchunes, and stopped on the south side of this point. All day we went about five hours, all by oar, the sea being calm. The Island of Los Angeles and the points of Huchunes and Abastos form a double bay. That on the side of the Port [i.e., San Francisco], the big one, has eight islands, most of which are small. One of them must be passed in sailing to the point of the Huchunes. It has a sandbar and must be passed a little distant to the west. It is noticeable only at low tide and on the western side is entirely covered with trees.

October 16. We left the said point of the Huchunes, which we called San Pablo. Where we slept there is a beach good as a camping place, with water and firewood. This Point San Pablo has opposite it another point which we called San Pedro, and between them are two little islands. From one point to the other might be twice the distance from the fort to the opposite shore [i.e., across the Golden Gate]. These two points enclose the bay as we have said, and form another one, much larger, which we estimate to be 4 leagues from the center to the periphery. This bay is square in shape. On the north and west it has 5 rancherias which are still unconverted. On the western side is a cove which, according to the Indians, is quite large. But Alferez Gabriel Moraga has explored it twice, on the expeditions he has made to those parts.

At a league and a half we encountered another headland, which we called San Andres [i.e., Point Pinole]. Between the latter and that of San Pablo, all mainland of San José, is an estuary which terminates in a stream [i.e., mouth of San Pablo Creek] which, according to those who have been there and to the Indians, is like that of the pueblo, except that it is deeper and is well wooded. From one point to the other the depth of the water is four varas, becoming shallower to two, when one sails close to the shore. Farther into the bay conditions would be the same as at the port for there is a channel which carries a considerable current. This is all the land of the Huchunes. It is quite bare, although there are some oak trees.

As far as the strait of the Karquines, including what we have covered yesterday and today, we must have spent about eight hours, all to the northeast, one-quarter north from the Mission. Here ends the above mentioned bay, estimated at 8 leagues. The strait is formed by an island [i.e., Mare Island] and the mainland of San José. The island soon ends and is replaced by mainland on both sides. The strait runs to the southwest and makes a half-turn to the south. It carries a heavy current, depending on the rise and fall of the tide. This strait is about two and a half leagues long and about a quarter of a league wide, in some places somewhat wider. It ends in the land of the Chupunes, where it becomes broader. Here we stopped at half-past eleven o'clock at a little beach which is dry at low tide and where the boats have to retreat 200 varas in order not to be stranded. Here at low tide is seen a rock, which otherwise is covered with water and which might damage the boats on landing. However, a little farther down toward the hill is a sort of little valley, which is good. This place we called la Division [probably at or near Martinez]. It has a large pool of water and plenty of firewood. Here we passed the night without incident. The shore of the strait of the Karquines which is opposite the mainland of San José is very barren.

October 17. [The party entered the delta.]

ABORIGINAL GROUPS

With the Viader and Abella diaries the formal documentary descriptions of Costanoan people and territory east of San Francisco come to an end. Nevertheless, there are certain other sources which convey information of use to the ethnographer. These are, first, some of the accounts left by travelers, particularly those by Chamisso and Choris in 1816 (translated by A. C. Mahr, 1932); second, the vocabularies and discussion of linguistics written by Fray Felipe Arroyo de la Cuesta (1837); third, the transcripts of the Mission baptism books made by Pinart (no date); forth, the accumulated habitation site records of the California Archaeological Survey. These sources will be used here for further examination of the location of the aboriginal groups concerned and their population.

LOCATION

The subordinate divisions of the natives inhabiting Alameda and Contra Costa counties can probably be allocated to five primary geographical areas. Some of these can be associated with reasonably well recognized names; some cannot. They may be briefly considered.

Area 1. The Alameda. —From Milpitas north to approximately Richmond, and west of the hills, the early expeditions (Fages, Anza) found numerous rancherias, as previously mentioned. The Sal-Danti party in 1795, covering the southern half of this area thoroughly, found almost no native inhabitants. An originally fair-sized population therefore must have been dispersed nearly completely in twenty years.

No general, regional name was ever applied to these Indians, but a few individual rancheria names have been preserved. These are all designated in the San Francisco Baptism Book as lying on the "otra banda del estero" (or some similar expression):

1778:	paraje	Halchis
1779:	paraje	Chapugtac
	paraje	Tupucantche
1780:	rancheria	Genau (or Chynau)

	rancheria	Tupine
1780:	rancheria	Itenau
	rancheria	Tumiamac
1781:	rancheria	Torqui
1782:	rancheria	Putnatac
	rancheria	Ocquizara
	rancheria	Tacomui
1784:	rancheria	Ssichitca
	araje	Cosopo
1786:	rancheria	Ilorocrochay
	paraje	Guet

These records show, first, that from 1778 to 1786 the missionaries from San Francisco recognized fifteen inhabited places along the southeast shore of the Bay. Second, it is very clear that active search for converts was proceeding during these eight years Finally, the field must have been substantially exhausted because none of the fifteen localities are noted after 1786.

Nevertheless, San Francisco did not get all the natives, because Santa Clara was much closer and was active during the same period Unfortunately we cannot determine the village of origin for these neophytes, since the baptism book (according to Pinart's transcript) allocates the individual converts to rancherias, not according to the native names of the latter, but by corresponding Saint's names, which must have been applied, Mexican fashion, by the local missionaries Only after 1801 did Santa Clara change its system, and of course by this time no heathen Indians remained locally.

San José was founded and began conversions in 1797. The baptism book here has the converts identified according to general area, not specific village. There are six such regions, or categories: "Palos colorados," "de la Alameda," "del Estero," "del Norte," "del Este," "del Sur." Of these the first three are evidently local and in the region now being discussed: (1) the redwoods back of Oakland and San Leandro; (2) Alameda Creek and adjacent plain; (3) the shore of the Bay directly west of the mission. The conversions, 1797-1802 inclusive, from these three areas were respectively 31, 170, 130, indicating that San Francisco and Santa Clara had by no means completed the conquest.

Area 2. The coast from Richmond to Carquinez Strait.—That this strip was held by the tribal group known as Huchiun (Cuchillones, Juchillones) has been supported by the accounts of Amador (diary of 1797) and of Abella (diary of 1811). The latter writer, it will be remembered, renamed the Point of the Huchines, Point San Pablo, a name which it retains today. The point of the Abastos or Aguastos became Point San Pedro. The Abastos, it may be pointed out, were neither Costanoan nor resident on the east side of the Bay. They lived on the Bay shore of Marin County, as is abundantly evident from the San Francisco baptism records.

The Huchiun are mentioned by Chamisso and by Choris (Mahr, 1932) in 1816, jointly with various other North Bay tribes. Chamisso says that the Utschíun, together with the Guyment, Olumpalic, Soclan, and Sonomi, all speak the same language, a manifest error. Choris repeats the mistake. Arroyo de la Cuesta gives a Huichun vocabulary and says (1837; MS p. 21) "Karquin and Huichun is one language—Saclan is another, entirely distinct." The Huchiun are noted in the San Francisco records first in 1787 (Tuchiun) and subsequently repeatedly until 1809, although they never appear in the San José record. Apparently San José derived converts from the east rather than from up coast.

The exact limits of the Huchiun are doubtful. Amador spent a night somewhere near Richmond and then went north to find them. Abella associates them closely with Point San Pablo, and implies that their land reached as far as the strait. We may tentatively draw their boundary between Rodeo and Crockett.

Area 3. Carquinez Strait and Concord Valley.—We are dealing here with the shore line from Crockett through Martinez nearly to Pittsburg, and inland between Concord and Pacheco. The principal Indian name associated with this area is Karquin, from which the strait takes its name. Just what group of people is involved is a puzzling question.

Kroeber, in the Handbook of California Indians (1925, pp. 356, 466), includes the Karkin as a division of the southern Wintun, which would mean that the principal seat of habitation was north of the strait. While there is no evidence in the early records to exclude this completely, there is certainly no question that at least a portion of the group lived on the south side. Thus the mission records before the settlement of the north shore report numerous baptisms of Karquines or Tarquines. Viader (1810) camped near Martinez, where the rancheria of the Tauquines used to be. Arroyo de la Cuesta says the language of the Karkin is the same as (or similar to) that of the Huchiun. The latter is Costanoan: the former could not be Wintun. The name Karkin was said by Arroyo de la Cuesta to signify "trocar," or "to trade." It has been supposed that the reference is to the rancheria which traded with Cañizares and other early explorers.

The Karquines (on the south side at least) probably began near Crockett, adjoining the Huchiun on the west. The next sure tribe on the east is the Julpunes, whose western limit is near Antioch and who must be considered a delta people.

Abella (1811) states that the strait ends on the east in the land of the Chupunes, and on the strength of this statement Schenck (1926) places the Chupunes from Port Costa to Martinez. Schenck also cites Father Narciso Duran who, in 1817, mentions the Chupcanes as holding this territory. Yet Viader, in 1810, says it was the site of the former rancheria of the Karquines.

The mission records are illuminating. San Francisco reports its first baptism of a Karquin in 1787. The statement reads: "natural de la otra banda del paraje de Turis, ó nacion Karquin." The next reference is in 1801 when eleven of this "nation" were baptized. In the meantime, scores of Huchiun had been baptized. In 1810, Chupunes or Chupanes (or Chupkanes) begin to appear, both at San Francisco and San José. This looks as if missionization moved progressively north and east along the shore: first the Huchiun, then the Karkin, then the Chupunes, and finally the Julpunes, who begin to show up at San José in significant numbers in 1811.

This concept of the original status of aboriginal units in northern Contra Costa County is at variance with the arrangement postulated by Schenck, who places the "Tarquimenes" and the "Tarquimes" eastward across the delta islands nearly to Stockton. There is some reason to believe that many of these delta islands were aboriginally uninhabited, but wholly apart from this consideration, another explanation can be offered, which has been suggested by Schenck (1926) and by the present writer (1955). It rests upon the probability that many of the delta tribes had undergone extensive migration, owing to Spanish military pressure in the period from 1785 to 1810. Thus the Karquines of the early accounts may have moved east along the south shore of Suisun Bay, far into the delta, and hence may have been recorded by later visitors under a series of name variants. In the meantime the Chupunes, or Chupkanes, may have been pushed southwest, as intimated by Kotzebue (cited by Schenck, 1926, p. 130). It is pretty clear that the tribal territories as reported by a succession of explorers from 1805 to 1820 did not conform to the aboriginal pattern. Our best solution, for present purposes, is to consider the strip from Crockett to Port Chicago as having been the range of the Karkin.

Area 4. The interior valleys from Lafayette to Walnut Creek and Danville. — Part of this region was traversed by Fages and Crespi, who reported several villages. It is later identified as the home of the Saclanes. This tribal aggregate first comes into prominence in 1795 in connection with the murder of the San Francisco Christians, who slept on the beach and reached the Saclanes by noon. Amador, on his expedition of 1797, reached them in less than twenty-four hours from Mission San José. Other documents, cited previously, indicate that in spite of terminal disorganization and scattering the original home of the group was in the small valleys west of Mt. Diablo.

The linguistic evidence adduced by Arroyo de la Cuesta (1837) demonstrates that the Saclanes were a non-Costanoan people, perhaps related to the Plains Miwok. This identification as Miwok, was first made, on the basis of the de la Cuesta vocabulary, by A. S. Gatschett, was verified by C. Hart Merriam, and first published by M. S. Beeler (1955). Kroeber (1925) classes Saclan as doubtfully Costanoan, but shows the group as Costanoan on his large colored tribal map. Regardless of their linguistic affiliation, however, historically and ecologically they must be considered as in the same position as the Costanoans who surrounded them.

The mission records are explicit. The tribe, at least under the usual name, was converted at the San Francisco Mission and no other. The first baptisms occurred in 1794 and the last in 1798.

Area 5. The interior valleys from Livermore to Dublin and Pleasanton. —This territory was barely skirted on the west by Fages and Crespi and on the east by Anza and Font, none of whom left any record of native villages. In fact, no data in the correspondence or diaries are of significance except the reference, cited previously, to the rancheria of the Asirines. We have, on the other hand, some suggestive information from the baptism books of the mission at San José.

Until 1803 converts were identified in the San José records largely by direction. Thus three of the categories were "del Norte," "del Este," "del Sur." Of these, "del Este" seems to point to the Livermore Valley and nearby arroyos as the most likely inhabited region. In 1803, the rancheria, or some other type of ethnic name, is substituted. From 1803 to 1808, all converts were drawn from twelve places having recognizable names, ending in -*an*, -*en*, -*in*, or -*un*, characteristic Costanoan word endings. None of these places can be identified as connected with the foothill or plains area bordering the Bay. None are Saclan—to the northwest of the Livermore Valley—since that group was extinct by 1798. None can be referred to the San Joaquin Valley, since no serious conversions were attempted there, as indicated by the baptism book, before 1809. Consequently these places must have been in the interior valleys, east and northeast of Mission San José.

The names are as follows: Saoan, Ssouyen, Seunen, Irgin, Pelnen, Asirin, Causen (or Cusscun), Tannan (Annan), Caburun (Calenrun, Carurun), Zuicun, Tuibun, Julien. The first three are clearly synonyms, and refer to the tribe often called Seunenes. The others might perhaps have been rancherias subordinate to this tribal group, but such an hypothesis is negated by the rancheria Asirin, which is referred to in the documents relating to the Cuevas affair as if it had an independent status. Therefore, there were apparently several independent villages in the area as a whole.

POPULATION ESTIMATES

Since we have no other information and since there is no obvious tribal designation associated with the region, the geographical description will have to suffice to designate the area.

The aboriginal population of the East Bay was tentatively estimated from the village counts of the Fages and Anza expeditions as 2,400 and 2,150, respectively. It is possible to arrive at a new and independent estimate by means of the mission statistics.

The missionaries, or their agents, entered the area in question and sought converts to Christianity, who were immediately baptized and entered in the mission archive as Christians. Alameda and Contra Costa counties, except for the extreme eastern border in the San Joaquin Valley, were completely Christianized by 1810. Theoretically, therefore, the total baptisms should equal the population. However, during the process of conversion a serious population decline was in progress for other reasons. Disease, fugitivism to the deep interior, depression of the birth rate, economic and social upheaval, military butchery, all took such a toll of the nonmissionized, or surviving, Indians that certainly no more than one-half of the aboriginal number could have been actually baptized. At all events, the total number of baptisms represents a subminimal estimate of population.

The baptisms are here tabulated according to the mission and according to the five areas described previously. No attempt is made to segregate the entries by year, since we are interested in the total, not the annual increment. Certain particular problems deserve comment.

The San Francisco record is very precise, since it allocates each neophyte to his rancheria, or at least to the local region of his origin. Santa Clara, however, as noted previously, gives no indication of the origin before 1805. By this time, all the local natives had been exhausted and only valley tribes are mentioned. It is probable that from 1777 to 1789 the natives in the immediate vicinity were being converted. From 1790 to 1801, inclusive, 1,392 baptisms of gentiles were recorded. Some of these came from the south and the southwest, some from the hills to the east, and probably some represented early conquests in the San Joaquin Valley. Many, however, must have come from the north and northeast, in particular, before the foundation of San José in 1797. A conservative guess for this fraction would be 400, and this figure will be adopted.

San José, from 1797 to 1802 inclusive, indicates the origin of its converts only by general area or direction, as previously pointed out. Some arbitrary allocation is demanded. Hence, as a reasonable solution, those natives from "Palos colorados," "de la Alameda," "del Estero," and "del Sur" are assigned to area 1. Those from "del Norte" are considered Huchiun and those "del Este" are allocated to area 5. After 1802, the San José records specify the villages, which are all from area 5. The tabulated totals are shown at bottom of page.

The total for San Francisco and San José equals 1,848 baptisms. Adding an estimated 400 for Santa Clara makes 2,248. This figure, which has to be regarded as a minimum for population since it covers only mission baptisms from the region, is as great as the estimates based on the expeditions of the first decade of settlement, and proves beyond question that those estimates were highly conservative. If we assume that the aboriginal population was twice the value of the baptisms, the total would have reached 4,496. If it be allowed that conversion close to the missions was exceptionally rapid and thorough, a somewhat lower figure may be accepted, say 3,000. This estimate, however, must be regarded as the lowest consistent with the known facts.

	Area 1	Area 2	Area 3	Area 4	Area 5	Total
San Francisco	33	206	211	297	15	762
Santa Clara						400
San José	347	136			603	1,086
Total	380	342	211	297	618	2,248

Although little direct information pertaining to population can be secured, it is nevertheless interesting to consider the prehistoric sites in the East Bay which have been noted by California archaeologists. Most of those which can be regarded as habitation mounds have been recorded by the University of California Archaeological Survey, and have been plotted on map 1.

It must not be thought that each site represented on the map by a dot was inhabited in 1769, or the years immediately preceding, for many of the mounds are known to have been formed during the Middle Culture period, which antedated modern times by several centuries. The chief physical characteristic of these accumulations is the very high content of mussel, and to some extent clam, shell. From this feature it has been deduced that at one time a very large population existed along the shore of the Bay.

The record of known sites, as shown on map 1, is valuable, not as an indication of the size of population, but rather of its distribution. Admitting that perhaps the majority of the sites along the Bay shore from San Leandro to Crockett were abandoned before 1770, it is still apparent that the areas designated on the map as Alamedan and Huchiun contained a heavy concentration of inhabited spots. This conclusion is in conformity with the waterfront habitat and the probable large food reserves. Along the strait and the southern shore of Suisun Bay the known habitation mounds are less numerous, but there are enough to indicate a reasonably high population density. This area on the map has been ascribed to Karquin.

Through the generally hilly interior of Alameda and Contra Costa counties there are but two areas of sizable extent in which preconquest village sites occur with relative frequency. One is the Lafayette-Walnut Creek-Danville region and the other the Livermore Valley, west to Pleasanton and Dublin. These provinces were inhabited in the late eighteenth century by the Saklan and Seunen respectively, and are so designated on the map. Indeed, the correspondence between archaeological sites and the occurrence of rancherias in early colonial times is remarkably close. The conclusion is permissible that the pattern of occupancy found by the Spaniards had been established long previously and was fully stabilized at the time of their arrival. This condition in turn argues a mature balance between the natural environment and the indigenous population.